Delivered from Transsexual Sin

Michael Fernandez

ISBN 979-8-88616-541-8 (paperback)
ISBN 979-8-88616-542-5 (digital)

Christian Faith Publishing
832 Park Avenue
Meadville, PA 16335
www.christianfaithpublishing.com

Printed in the United States of America

Power of the Cross and Resurrection Set Me Free and Healed Me

INTRODUCTION

The Lord that delivered me out of the paw of the lion, and out of the paw of the bear, He will deliver me out of the hand of this Philistine.(1 Samuel 17:32–37)

I realized that I had to reminisce on the mercies of God. I recalled how God healed me twice as a child and how, now, facing the uncircumcised philistine, He would heal me from the disease called Evans syndrome. Evans syndrome is an autoimmune disease in which an individual's antibodies attack their own red blood cells and platelets. This disease was causing my spleen to attack my blood cells and destroy my blood platelets. A normal platelet count ranges from 150,000 to 450,000. Due to the effects of this disease, my count was 3. My blood was so thin, it was dripping out of my nose and ears. I was unable to take baths because blood would pour out from under my nails and pores, limiting me to only showers. I had developed black blisters on my tongue the size of quarters due to the blood trying to escape out from my tongue. I was literally bleeding to death. The doctors were amazed that I was still alive. I should have been dead. The force of gravity alone should have caused all of my blood to have been expelled from my body, yet I was alive. As David said, 1 Samuel 17, "The Lord that delivered me out of the paw of the lion, and out of the paw of the bear, He will deliver me out of the hand of this Philistine." Everyone runs across a Goliath in their life. You would think that this was my Goliath, but it was not. I faced a greater Goliath in *How the Lord Set Me Free from Transsexual Sin.*

CONTENTS

Chapter 1

Healing Mercies of God at Age 7

I can recall feeling the first healing mercies of God at the young age of seven. I had developed a severe toothache, which caused my mouth to swell up twice its normal size. The swelling was so severe that it looked as though I had mumps. Growing up, we did not have money for medical or dental care, so I was unable to receive medical attention. The entire side of my face was throbbing, and the pain was so severe that I was unable to attend school. The pain kept me up all night. This went on for days. I awoke at about 3:00 a.m. on a cold morning unable to sleep due to the pain. I got up and walked around the house, hoping that the cold air would somehow calm the pain. As I was walking around the house, crying due to the extent of the pain, I cried out to Jesus and asked Him to take the pain away from me. As I did this, the pain was immediately gone, and the swelling went down instantly. I believe this was the healing mercy of God. According to the Word of God, "Ask, and it shall be given you; seek, and ye shall find; knock, and it shall be opened unto you" (Matthew 7:7 KJV). God is not a respecter of persons that he would even answer the prayer of a child.

Healing Mercy of God at Age 15

Reminiscing on another healing mercy of God, I am reminded of when God healed my back. At the age of fifteen, while in karate class, I hurt my back flipping another student onto a mat. The pain was so severe that any part of my body that was touched ignited the pain in my back. I remember I would put a sixteen-ounce Coca-Cola bottle under my back so that the shape of it would offer some relief from the pain. It was difficult to dress myself and to even put my shoes on. Mornings and afternoons were extremely difficult as I had to walk to and from school. I moved around like I was eighty years old.

I remember John Osteen quoting Isaiah 53:5, "But He was wounded for our transgression, He was bruised for our iniquities: the chastisement of our peace was upon Him; and with His stripes we are healed." I began speaking and confessing these words, "By His stripes, I am healed!"

The devil would put negative thoughts in my mind, telling me, "You're lying! "You're not healed! You're still in pain!" He would try to attack and steal the Word of God from my heart in order to steal my faith, but I stood firm.

I had to rebuke him daily, stand fast in my faith, and believe that what God's word said was true. As the word of God says, "Let the weak say I'm strong" (Joel 3:10 KJV).

The severe pain and fighting the good fight of faith went on for four months. I remember one day while sitting at my desk in school, another student turned and said that he could tell by looking in my eyes that I was in so much pain. I responded to him by saying, "No matter if I look like I'm in pain and no matter if I walk as though I'm in pain, by His stripes I am healed." According to the Word of God in Hebrews 11:1, "Now FAITH is the substance of things hoped for, the evidence of things not seen." This showed me that faith is believing the word of God even though you don't feel or see the results. Faith is believing that it is done. It is the key to unlocking what was already given to us. Healing was already given to us by Jesus Christ. All that we have to do is reach out and accept it in faith. Faith is not making God heal me. Faith is just the key to healing mercies that were already done at the cross. I claimed that healing was already mine, and I rested in that. I didn't feel like I was healed, but I didn't let my feelings control me. At that moment, I realized that the five senses were the enemies of my faith. I didn't go by feelings; I went by the Word of God.

Our church threw a Christmas party that December for the youth, and it was being hosted by my Sunday school teacher. During the party, all the youth were outside playing. I was watching them play, wishing the pain was gone so I could join them. I was telling myself how I wish I could play with them like I used to. Then the Lord spoke to me audibly and said, "Son, don't you believe your prayers?" I responded and said, "Yes, Jesus." He said, "Go to your Sunday school teacher, and tell her not to pray for your healing, but to praise Me for the healing already given to you at the cross." I went to my Sunday school teacher and relayed to her what Jesus had told me to do. She sat me down on the chair, and we began to praise the Lord. As we did this, the pain left me immediately, and I was able to bend down for the first time in four months! I then went outside to play with the other teenagers. Thank God for His healing mercies.

EVANS SYNDROME

It all started in April of 2010. I recall walking into a Bible study that day and not knowing anyone there. As soon as I sat down, the minister who was preaching called out to me. I didn't realize at the time that he was a true prophet. He said to me, "Young man, stand up," as he began to prophesy over me. He prophesied that I would be preaching the Gospel of Jesus Christ on television and radio. He also spoke about how Jesus had delivered me from transexual sin and that God had set me free from that lifestyle. He said that I had backslid and how God had delivered me for this specific time to help set people who are bound by that demon of homosexuality during these last days of evil. He shared that I must be bold with my testimony because so many in the church say they are Christians yet they live that lifestyle. He then prophesied that the devil didn't want me to testify and was going to try to kill me with a rare disease, Evans syndrome. He stated that God said to be bold and of good courage and not to fear because He will see me through. He told me not to worry because God was going to protect my life and I would not lose my house. Everything that this prophet prophesied came to pass.

This is how it all started; I woke up one morning, and blood started to come out of my nose, but I ignored it. Then all of a sudden, black blisters the size of a quarter appeared on my tongue, and I went to my primary doctor. I began to feel very weak, and he diagnosed me with low blood platelets and thinning blood, so much so that I was bleeding to death. At first, I didn't want to believe, but I remembered what the prophet said about the devil trying to kill me because he didn't want me to share my testimony of how Jesus set me free from homosexual sin. The devil did not want me to share with transexuals that they can be set free by knowing the true Gospel of Jesus Christ. At the time I began to fear, but I realized that God doesn't give us the spirit of fear. I began to speak the Word of God, and I began to quote scripture day and night. "For God hath not given us the spirit of fear; but of power, and of love and sound mind" (2 Timothy 1:7). I began to speak to that mountain of disease, to die and to be cast into the sea. I'm not saying that I did not feel weak and in pain, but I did not confess it so. Instead, I confessed that I was healed.

According to Joel 3:10, "Let the weak say, 'I am strong.'" Believe me, it wasn't easy confessing the word. I sometimes felt that I was lying through my teeth. I remember what the Bible said, "*Let the weak say that they are strong.*" I took that to mean that we must declare that we are strong even if I didn't feel it at the time. I realized again, that our sense of taste, smell, hearing, touching, and seeing are the enemies of our faith.

According to Isaiah 53:5, "And with stripes we are healed." I am healed no matter if I felt sick or weak, even when blood began to come from under my fingernails or when the doctors were telling me that chemo treatment wasn't working on me. I stood on God's word no matter how

I felt. When Satan was telling me to go ahead and give up, I rebuked him and stood against all his lies."

According to the scripture of St. Mark 11:22–23,

> And Jesus answering saith unto them, Have faith in God. For verily I say unto you, That whosoever shall say unto this mountain, Be thou cast in the sea; and shall not doubt in his heart, but shall believe that those things which he saith shall come to pass; he shall have whatsoever he saith.

I realize that God was expecting me to speak to my mountains and exercise the authority that was given to the believers. We need to speak to our mountains of sickness and fear because Jesus Christ already healed and blessed us on the cross. It is up to us not to accept anything when the devil is trying to steal from our lives because Jesus has given us the weapons to fight a good fight of faith.

I was at my home at the time, and I called the ambulance service, and they picked me up. As I was in the ambulance, I started to witness to the paramedic the goodness of God and how God saved me. The power of conviction came upon him. I told him that God will forgive anyone of his sins, and his response was that he didn't think God could forgive him because he was a devil worshiper. I told him that he needed to repent. At that moment, he began to cry and repent and accept Jesus as his Lord and Savior. Also at that same moment, I began to tell the devil, "You will not be able to take me down without a fight, that I am going to take as many as with me to heaven."

As soon as I got to the hospital, they gave me all kinds of tests. Thank God that I didn't get AIDS from the lifestyle I used to live. The doctors put me under chemo treatment in the morning. The treatments lasted approximately four hours. I was in the hospital for two and a half months, and I was witnessing to the people in the hospital, even to the doctors leading them to the Lord. Every day I would get scriptures and put them on the walls and would repeat the following words: by the stripes of Jesus Christ, I am healed. I believed these words in my mind and in my heart.

Because the word of God said in **Philippians 4:6–8,**

> **Be careful for nothing: (that means don't worry about anything no matter what doctors reports say) it continues saying but in every thing by prayer and supplication with thanksgiving let your request be made known unto God. And the peace of God, which passeth all understanding, shall keep your hearts and minds through, Christ Jesus. Finally, brethren, whatsoever things are true, whatsoever things are honest, whatsoever things are just, whatsoever things are pure, whatsoever things are lovely, whatsoever things are of good report; if there be any praise, think on these things.**

When doubt or fear started to come into my mind, I remembered that we are fighting a spiritual battle as long as we are in this world. We are going to have to fight the good fight of faith. We have to tell all sickness that it doesn't have the right to stay in our bodies. As the scripture said, we are not fighting against flesh and blood, but we are fighting evil spirits of fear, principalities, and words of doubt.

I realize that I had to fight this sickness and remind the devil that Jesus already healed me and that he was already defeated. I realize I had to put on the armor of God. In **Ephesians 6:10–12,**

> **Finally, my brethren, be strong in the Lord, and in the power of his might. Put on the whole armour of God, that ye may be able to stand against the wiles of the devil. For we wrestle not against flesh and blood, but against principalities, against powers, against the rulers of the darkness of this world, against spiritual wickedness in high places.**

I started to quote the scripture and meditate day and night in the Word. I didn't listen to the doubt, fear, or negative reports from the doctors. At times blood would ooze out from under my fingernails. The doctors were saying that the chemo treatments I was receiving were not working. I told the doctors that Jesus is still on his throne and that he has the final say-so about my life and health. I confessed to the doctor that I was healed by the stripes of Jesus. I'm sure the doctor thought I was going crazy. I didn't let the negative report get to me; I just continued to cast down every evil imagination that came against my faith.

According to **2 Corinthians 10:3–5,**

> **For though we walk in the flesh, we do not war after the flesh; For the weapons of our warfare are not carnal, but mighty through God to the pulling down of strong holds; Casting down imaginations, and every high thing that exalteth itself against the knowledge of God, and bringing into captivity every thought to the obedience of Christ.**

I started to stand on the Word of God and attack the devil with the sword of the spirit and full armor, which is the Word of God.
According to I Peter 1:24,

> **Who his own self bare our sins in his own body on the tree, that we, being dead to sins, should live unto righteousness: by whose stripes ye were healed.**

Every day, after treatment, I would sneak out of the hospital and have my roommate pick me up to go home to see my little dogs because I missed them a lot. When I snuck out, I would go to buy some shorts and T-shirts because I disliked the clothes the hospital gave us to use. They had to wash the clothes I bought in my room with body wash and hang them up to dry, but I had to be careful not to let my hands stay in the water too long because the blood would start to come out from under my fingernails.

The doctors and staff couldn't understand why I bought my own clothes and refused to wear the hospital garments. They joked about how they felt as though they were walking in the flea market because my room had the scent of body wash from all the clothes hanging on the clothesline that I had made. They asked why I didn't like the hospital clothes. I responded by telling them that I like wearing my T-shirt and short pants while I was in the hospital because I wasn't planning on staying in the hospital. I was planning on going home. The treatment went on for two months. One day, the Lord spoke to me in an audible voice. He told me to leave the hospital and go to church to have Dodie Osteen pray for me. I wanted to leave, but the doctors told me I couldn't leave because I could die at any minute. I told the doctors, "God has the final say-so about my life. Death, sickness, and the devil have no say-so over me." "I shall not die, but live, and declare the works of the LORD" (Psalm 118:17).

I held on to my confession of faith. I told the doctors to take the IV out of my arms, and if not, I was walking out with it still in my arms. The doctors strongly advised against it. I told them, "Don't worry, I'm in my Father's hands." I called my brother in the Lord to come and pick me up. As I started down the hospital hall, while pulling my oxygen tank, all fear and doubt attacked me. I refused to let fear take over. As I got to the church parking lot, I asked the Lord to give me the strength to walk into the church. I asked one of the ushers to ask Dodie Osteen to please pray for me. They took me up to the front of the church, and she prayed for me. That night, Jesus visited me in a vision. He stood at the entry of my bedroom door, and He said to me, "Tell the church that I am coming, and that I love them." He further said, "Son, you are going to live to preach in last days."

That morning, the hospital called me and said that they had a new drug that could help my platelet count increase and could help stop the bleeding. Remember, I already went through several chemo treatments and drugs that didn't help. I told the doctors that if Jesus wants to heal me through doctors or a miracle, His will would be done. I believed He was going to heal me. I went to the hospital, and they gave me the chemo treatment drug, and praise God, it stabilized my blood. I continued with this treatment for several months until I was strong enough to endure the surgery to remove my spleen that was attacking my platelets.

I told the doctor that I knew they had done their best to keep me alive. But I thank Jesus for healing me through the power of prayer.

C HAPTER 2

QUESTIONS REGARDING UNANSWERED PRAYER

People ask, "Why didn't God answer my prayer regarding my loved one that was sick they were so young?" They told me, "They had faith, that they confessed the promises of God's word on healing, and that they even had healing evangelists pray for them, but they still pass away."

We know that these questions that we have regarding unanswered prayers cannot be answered by anyone other than God. If He wishes to let you know, He will. All I have are words of encouragement. All God asks from his children is to have faith and trust in Him. We must realize that God's word says in Hebrews 11:6 (KJV), *"And without faith it is impossible to please him, for he who cometh to God must believe that he is, and that he is a rewarder of them that diligently seek him."*

If you feel your prayer wasn't answered, know that it was but on the other side of heaven. You will see your loved one healed and completely whole again. You are like the heroes of faith that endured till the end. "Blessed is the man that endureth temptation: for when he is tried, he shall receive the crown of life, which the Lord hath promised to them that love him" (James 1:12 KJV).

Look at the heroes of faith that went before you. They may not have seen their promises until they got to heaven. "All of these people died in faith without receiving the promises, but they saw the promises from a distance and welcomed them. They confessed that they were strangers and immigrants on earth" (Hebrews 11:13 CEB).

WHY THEIR LIVES WERE SHORTENED AS CHRISTIANS

Regarding your loved ones and why their life was shortened, young or old alike, why did tragedy strike when they were living for the Lord? What happens to angles? I thought they were supposed to protect us?

I realize that there are a lot of UNANSWERED QUESTIONS. Why did it happen? We will all be able to ask Jesus when we see him.

According to John 10:10,

> The thief cometh not, but for to steal, and to kill,
> and to destroy; I have come that they might have
> life, and that they might have it more abundantly.

Let's look at one of the great servants of the Lord, Job. How did he deal with all the suffering? According to Job 1:2, "He had seven sons and three daughters."

> While he was still speaking, yet another messenger came and said, "Your Sons and daughters were feasting and drinking wine at the oldest brother house, when suddenly a mighty wind swept in from the desert and struck the four corners of the house. It collapsed on them and they are dead, and I am the only one who has escaped to tell you." (Job 1:18–19)

Then said his wife unto him, Dost thou still retain thine integrity? Curse God, and die. But he said unto her, Thou speakest as one

of the foolish women speaketh. What? Shall we receive good at the hand of God, and shall we not receive evil? IN ALL THIS DID NOT JOB SIN WITH HIS LIPS? (Job 2:9–10)

Here we see that JOB was facing CHAOS in his life but he didn't give up and he didn't curse the Lord. According to **Romans 8:18,** "FOR I CONSIDER THAT THE SUFFERINGS OF THIS PRESENT TIME ARE NOT WORTH COMPARING WITH THE GLORY THAT WILL BE REVEALED TO US."

As St. Paul said, according to **Romans 8:36 (ISV),**

For your sake we are being put to death all day long, We are thought of as sheep headed for slaughter.

According to Psalm 23:1–6, "The Lord is my shepherd; I shall not want. He maketh me to lie down in green pastures he leadeth me beside the still waters. He restoreth my soul: he leadeth me in the paths of righteousness for his name's sake. Yea, though I walk through the valley of the shadow of death, I will fear no evil: for thou art with me; thy rod and thy staff they comfort me. Thou preparest a table before me in the presence of mine enemies: thou anointest my head with oil; my cup runneth over. Surely goodness and mercy shall follow me all the days of my life: I and I will dwell in the house of the Lord for ever."

WHY IS ONE BORN SICK OR BORN WITH HOMOSEXUAL DESIRES

I'd like to clear the minds of the believers regarding sickness, such as down syndrome, no arms, legs, or with both sexes (hermaphrodites), and homosexual desires. This is what the Lord Jesus revealed to me through his word. Not all homosexuals are born with these desires. Some are abused, or some just experimented not realizing they were opening the door to demons of perversion.

The first thing I'd like to share with you is that God didn't put any sickness on you to teach you something in life. How could it be that the God that died on the cross to heal you and set you free from all sin would then put sickness on you? Let's look at this scripture.

According to Romans 5:12,

> Where, as by one man's sin entered into the world, and death by sin; and so death passed upon all men, for that all have sinned.

We can see from this scripture that you didn't have to do anything to become a sinner all you had to do is be born into this world. You were born in sin because of the first sin of Adam. You were born in the kingdom of Satan. Every person was born spiritually dead and separate from God because of Adam. Your spirit, DNA, and physical chemistry were contaminated by sin. Mankind was born spiritually dead in fulfilling the lust of the flesh as described in the Galatians

According to Galatians 5:19–21,

> Now the works of the flesh are manifest, which are these; Adultery, fornication, uncleanness, lasciviousness, Idolatry, witchcraft, hatred, variance, emulations, wrath, strife, seditions, heresies, Envyings, murders drunkenness, revellings, and such like: of the which I tell you before, as I have also told you in time past, that they which do such things shall not inherit the kingdom of God.

This explains why one is born in sickness, with no limbs, with down syndrome, born a hermaphrodite, or born with homosexual desires. It was because of Adam, not God.

God never made a sinner or made a person sick; it was because of Adam. God made a perfect man. If someone says that they were born a homosexual or sick because God is trying to teach them a lesson, it is a lie from the pit of hell. The reason they were born with those desires or born with sickness is because of Adam, not God. The scripture clearly stated, according to James 1:13, "Let no man say when he is tempted, I am tempted of God: for God cannot be tempted with evil, neither tempteth he any man."

IF YOUR SON SAYS HE WANTS TO BE A GIRL

This lady came to me and said that her son told her that he wanted to be a girl. I asked her what she told her son. She stated that she did not want to hurt his feelings. I responded, "So you want to spare his feelings?" If your child came to you and said that he had a drug problem, wouldn't you tell him that is not the right thing to do even if it hurt his feelings? Would you not try to register him in a rehab clinic? She responded, "Yes, I would tell him that it is wrong." I ask you, what is the difference?

She realized that she had to tell her child the truth. I am not telling you to condemn your son but to tell him the truth. He needs to know that God created him to be a boy and you should take the time to show him what the Word of God says regarding homosexual sin. It doesn't matter if he gets his feelings hurt or gets upset with you; remember, you are his parent. You, as the parent, should rebuke that homosexual spirit to stay away from your son in the name of Jesus. You should decree over your son in prayer every day that he is set free through the POWER OF THE CROSS AND THE RESURRECTION and that he is a new creature. According to 2 Corinthians 5:17 (KJV), "He is a new creature, old things are passed away behold, all things are become new." You don't beat your child you teach him the word God and show him that he was set free from all sin. Also explain to the child about temptation, evil suggestions, and lies that are from the devil. Young and old alike are going to be tempted. Teach them that they have power in Jesus's name to resist temptations.

As the scripture in Romans 15:1 says,

> We then that are strong ought to bear the infir-
> mities of the weak, and not to please ourselves.

I imagine that some of you may think that God will not forgive our sins because some of the things that we have done are shameful. If a person that committed fornication convinces themselves that it was a mistake. It wasn't a mistake, plans were made to meet that person. You even bought them flowers and candy and you made reservations with your credit card. This wasn't a mistake, it was all thought out and planned. Fall on your knees, and tell God the truth. Tell Him how you felt, tell Him that it felt good to your flesh. Confess your sins to the Father for He knows how you think and how you feel. Be honest and tell the Father, "I committed sin, and I am sorry in Jesus's name." Father, help me stand in believing in the power of the cross and resurrection that Jesus completed for my freedom from all sin.

God gives instructions in the old testament and also in the new testament when they are living in sin. These instructions should warn the righteous man and sinner. But I feel we should minister in love to correct our brothers in the Lord when they committed sin. I'd like to say, it is not a mistake it is called sin.

According to the scripture Ezekiel 3:17–21,

> Son of man I have made thee "a watchman unto
> the house of Israel: therefore hear the word at my
> mouth, and give them warning from me. When
> I say unto the wicked, Thou shalt surely die; and
> thou givest him not warning, nor speakest to
> warn the wicked from his wicked way, to save his
> life; the same wicked man shall die I his iniquity:
> but his blood will I require at thine hand. Yet if
> thou warn the wicked, and he turn not from his
> wickedness, nor from his wicked way, he shall die
> in his iniquity; but thou hast delivered thy soul.

Again, When a righteous man doth turn from his righteousness, and commit iniquity, and I lay a stumbling block before him, he shall die: because thou hast not given him warning he shall die I his sin, and his righteousness which he hath done shall to be remembered; but his blood will I require at thine hand. Nevertheless if thou warn the righteous man, that the righteous sin not, and he doth not sin, he shall surely live, because he is warned; also thou hast delivered thy soul.

This is an example from the New Testament, how God used Paul in chastening a brother in the church having a sexual relationship with his stepmother. Let's view this example from the Living Bible translation labeled "Paul Condemns Spiritual Pride."

According to Paul in 1 Corinthians 5:1–13 (NLT),

I can hardly believe the report about the sexual immorality going on among you—something that even pagans don't do. I am told that a man in your church is living in sin with his stepmother. You are so proud of yourselves, but you should be mourning in sorrow and shame. And you should remove this man from your fellowship.

Even though I am not with you in person, I am with you in the Spirit. And as though I were there, I have already passed judgment on this man in the name of the Lord Jesus. You must call a meeting of the church. I will be present with you in spirit, and so will the power of our Lord Jesus. Then you must throw this man out and hand him over to Satan so that his sinful nature will be destroyed and he himself will be saved on the day the Lord returns.

Your boasting about this is terrible. Don't you realize that this sin is like a little yeast that spreads through the whole batch of dough? Get rid of the old "yeast" by removing this wicked person from among you. Then you will be like a fresh batch of dough made without yeast, which is what you really are. Christ, our Passover Lamb, has been sacrificed for us. So let us celebrate the festival, not with the old bread of wickedness and evil, but with the new bread of sincerity and truth.

When I wrote to you before, I told you not to associate with people who indulge in sexual sin. But I wasn't talking about unbelievers who indulge in sexual sin, or are greedy, or cheat people, or worship idols. You would have to leave this world to avoid people like that. I meant that you are not to associate with anyone who claims to be a believer yet indulges in sexual sin, or is greedy, or worships idols, or is abusive, or is a drunkard, or cheats people. Don't even eat with such people.

It isn't my responsibility to judge outsiders, but it certainly is your responsibility to judge those inside the church who are sinning. God will judge those on the outside; but as the Scriptures say, "You must remove the evil person from among you."

Don't you realize that those who do wrong will not inherit the Kingdom of god? Don't fool yourselves. Those who indulge in sexual sin, or who worship idols, or commit adultery, or are male prostitutes, or practice homosexuality, or are thieves, or greedy people, or drunkards, or are abusive, or cheat people—none of these will inherit the Kingdom of God. Some of you were once like that. But you were cleansed; you were made holy; you were made right with God by calling on the name of the Lord Jesus Christ and by the Spirit of our God.

The good news is that Jesus died so you can be set free from sin. Review the scriptures. (1 Corinthians 6: 9–11)

CHAPTER 3

POWER OF THE CROSS SET ME FREE

I was born into a family that had issues. My mother gave me to my grandmother who always liked to dress me like a little girl. She always wanted a little granddaughter. I recommend not to dress your sons like little girls; it creates confusion in their little minds. When she had to go out, she would leave me with a next-door neighbor. At the age of six, I was sexually abused by the babysitter. This went on for years. He wasn't the only adult who sexually abused me; there were several other individuals. One of those individuals liked to burn my feet with cigarettes because he liked hearing me scream. He would tell me that he would put me outside in a dark garage if I told anyone. This went on for several years.

And the age of thirteen, I was invited to Lakewood Church. I met Pastor John Osteen and his wife, Dodie Osteen. I really enjoyed going to church. I felt the love of God. Pastor John Osteen was like a father to me. I always looked forward to the weekend so that I could go to church because of the love I felt there. I accepted the Lord Jesus as Lord and the baptizing of the Holy Ghost in speaking tongues. Thank God for the power of the Holy Ghost because I was able to face the evil I went through living in my father's house because it was living in spiritual hell. I felt I stirred up the nest of demons.

I did not know my father and his sister believed in Satan. I don't think the other family members knew about this either. How did I find out? My father's sister came over to our home. I hadn't seen her for several years. I was outside working in the yard when she got out of the car. She looked at me and seemed to be upset with me. She asked me what in the world I was doing. I asked her what I did wrong. She said, "You accepted Jesus as your Lord and broke the curse over you and your family." I asked her what she meant. She proceeded to tell me that my father and she believed in Satan and that I should reject Jesus as my Lord and Savior.

I told her she was crazy, and she told me that she would send an evil spirit to the house. I told her, "In Jesus's name, get away from me." When I went into the house, my father said that he also believed in Satan and I was making a big mistake by believing in Jesus. I told him I wasn't making a mistake. Sometimes I would hear voices. You think I am crazy, I am not. I wasn't the only one hearing the voices talking to me. I remember when a family member stayed over one night in the same room. I saw the evil spirit who looked just like my father coming through the door. I wasn't the only one to hear the evil spirit yelling that he hated me because I had Jesus as my God. I rebuked that spirit in the name of Jesus Christ to leave and it left!

Here I was, at the young age of thirteen, going through all of this. At the time, I felt as though I was going crazy. Praise God, Jesus used to come and visit me through visions and dreams to teach me not to be afraid of these evil spirits. He taught me to use His name to rebuke those evil spirits. I am telling you, brothers and sisters in the Lord, the Holy Ghost was teaching me Himself how to battle against this kingdom of darkness! This is the reason I thank Jesus for the gifts of the Holy Ghost that protected me in this battle. This went on for several years until I left my father's house. He wanted those evil spirits in his home. As long as I stayed in my father's home, those spirits tried to attack me. Jesus always protected me from them. I couldn't go anywhere else to live because I was just a child. Jesus became my teacher as well as my savior, and He taught me, by the Holy Ghost, how to walk in the authority of the holy name of Jesus.

I also thank God for John Osteen, for teaching us we have power in the name of Jesus to cast out demons. He also had other ministers such as Kenneth Hagin and Evangelist Norvel Hayes come and teach us how not to be afraid of these evil spirits and how to deal with these demons. They were teaching the same thing the Holy Ghost was teaching me. This was vital confirmation to me as I was going through this war of principalities and powers in my youth. Thank God for Pastor John Osteen. He was not afraid to teach the church that we have authority in the name of Jesus!

As the years passed, I was able to grow in the Lord. I started to minister and was evangelizing for several years. At the age of eighteen, the Lord spoke to me in an audible voice when I was praying in my bedroom. He said that I would be going to school. I asked the Lord, "Are you saying that I would be going to Bible school?" I told the Lord that I didn't have the money for Bible school. He told me to go to Lakewood Church on Wednesday, and there would be a woman that would call me by name. He told me that she would say that He had sent her to pay for my Bible school and my apartment.

I continued ministering, and I was being tormented by homosexual demons. I never lived in homosexual sin while I was in ministry. At that time it was taboo to talk about homosexual desires with others. They didn't have good ministries like Celebrate Recovery at Lakewood. Today, many churches have ministries that help people with addictions and have an accountability partner that believes in the power of the cross and resurrection.

I left the ministry and the church because I felt I was being a hypocrite even if I wasn't actually committing the homosexual sin. I knew I was committing the sin with my heart and mind, so I felt like a hypocrite. According to Matthew 5: 28, "But I say unto you, That whosoever looketh on a woman to lust after her hath committed adultery with her in his heart." This also applies to homosexual desires toward men. At that time I started to live a transexual lifestyle and also started taking female hormones in order to continue the process of sinning, partying, and clubbing in straight clubs and gay clubs. I even had a significant other. I cannot continue the gory details of this lifestyle.

When I Committed Suicide

One morning, I woke up and the devil was telling me, "If you really love Jesus, you should kill yourself, that way you wouldn't continue living the transexual lifestyle of sin." I got hold of some pain medication and was going to take it all, but before I took the pills, I started to pray to Jesus. I told him that if I couldn't stop thinking of committing homosexual sin, I preferred death instead of hurting Him. I took the whole bottle, and as I took the pills, I was praying, Jesus please forgive me. As I was falling to the floor, I heard the audible voice of Jesus saying, "My son, you are not going to die, but you will live, and declare, my works."

Even after Jesus gave me a second chance, I didn't repent. I continued to live the transexual lifestyle of sin. I had dreams of me preaching the gospel, but I continued to ignore the dreams from the Lord for several more months.

When I Repented

I remember one particular dream I had was of the rapture. Jesus was coming for the church, and as I looked into his eyes, I felt that He wasn't pleased with my lifestyle of transexual sin. I woke up and realized that I had to make choice.

After this happened, I repented and renounced homosexual sin and asked Jesus to cleanse my heart from all the sins I committed. I also asked in my prayers that He show me how to walk through the victory that He paid on the cross and his resurrection. According to 1 Corinthians 1:18, "For the preaching of the cross is to them that perish foolishness; but unto us which are saved it is the power of God." We must believe in the power of the cross and resurrection.

Thank you, Jesus, for another chance in life. One shouldn't give up in life as I did by believing the lies of the devil. The devil made it sound like I was doing Jesus a favor by committing suicide. You don't have to die, because Jesus died on the cross for our sins and the resurrection already destroyed the works of the devil.

Chapter 4

My Journey In Reversing My Physical Body

I asked the Lord in prayer to help restore my body. I had nose surgery so it wouldn't look as masculine. I had started taking the female hormones that caused breasts to grow. It took several years for the hormone effect to stop working in my body. My breasts had grown, and now I needed them to return to normal. I had to stop wearing women's clothing but couldn't really wear men's clothing because with breasts, I would look odd. I began the transformation and stopped living in sexual sin. I asked the Lord to help me to go through reversing the physical change. Jesus spoke to my spirit and said, "Don't worry, son, I know your heart, and it will take time."

So I started to dress in men's clothes, but then I encountered another problem. I looked like a woman dressed in men's clothes. I remember I went to the men's restroom, and another man in the restroom went out and told the police officer that was working in the building that there was a woman in the men's restroom. The police officer went into the men's restroom and told me that If I don't get out of the men's restroom, he was going to take me to jail. I told him, "Sir, I am a man," and proceeded to hand him my driver's license. He stated that I looked like a woman and the picture on my driver's license looked like a woman, so I would have to go to the ladies' restroom because it was causing too much confusion. I was so embarrassed because I felt that everybody that was in the building heard this exchange with the police officer. My appearance today is not what it was several years ago. If you'd like to see before and after pictures, go to my website www.mfministries.net.

BREAKING THE TIES WITH THE SIGNIFICANT OTHER

I had to deal with my significant other. We had been in a relationship for five years. I prayed to Jesus to help me to love my significant other as my BROTHER and not as a LOVER. The first thing that I had to do was to ask him to leave my apartment. I was afraid to tell my significant other because he had a bad temper. I eventually told him that I repented of my homosexual sin, and he told me I was crazy.

I told him that he had to leave the apartment, but he didn't want to leave. It took several months to get him out, and it wasn't easy. While he was there, he tried to have sexual relations with me. I told him that we couldn't because I am God's property. I was no longer his or the devil's or myself; I was bought with a price. According to 1 Corinthians 6:20, "For ye are bought with a price: therefore glorify God in your body, and in your spirit which are God's." When he left the apartment, my flesh began to miss him, so I told my flesh to shut up because I died with Jesus on the cross and my flesh was crucified. I believed in the power of the CROSS AND HIS RESURRECTION. According to Romans 6:1–2, "What shall we say then? Shall we continue in sin, that grace may abound? God forbid. How shall we, that are dead to sin, live any longer therein?"

This is the reason that I recommend that every person who is dealing with any addiction have an accountability partner. Number 1, think that Jesus shows me the revelation of his Word because according to 1 Corinthians 15:34, "Awake to righteousness, and sin not." Understanding what righteousness means that you are in right standing and believing with all your heart and resting in what Jesus did for you on the cross and resurrection. Also according to 2 Corinthians 5:21, "For he hath made him to be sin for us, who knew no sin; that we might be made the righteousness of God in him." One needs to begin to believe in the power of the **cross, according to 1 Corinthians 1:20, "It please God by the foolishness of preaching to save them that believe."** Believing and resting in the finished work of the cross and the resurrection.

As Adam activated the law of sin and death, according to Romans 5:12, "Wherefore, as by one man's sin entered into the world, and death by sin; and so death passed upon men for that all have sinned." But according to the scripture, Jesus set us free from the law of sin and death. According to Romans 8:2, "For the law of the Spirit of life in Christ Jesus hath made me free from the law of sin and death."

My people are destroyed for lack of knowledge: because thou hast rejected knowledge (Hosea 4:6 KJV). I'm not talking about believing in knowledge, I'm talking about believing in the Word of God with your heart. According to Matthew 24:35 (KJV), "Heaven and earth will pass away, but My words will not pass away."

We are made righteousness, holy, justified, sanctified through the power of the CROSS AND THE RESURRECTION. According to EPHESIANS 1:3–6, "Blessed be the God and Father of our Lord Jesus Christ, who hath blessed us with all spiritual blessing in heavenly places in Christ: According as he hath chosen us in him before the foundation of the world, that we should be holy and without blame before him I love: Having predestinated us unto the adoption of children by Jesus Christ to himself, according to the good pleasure of this will. TO THE PRAISE OF HIS GLORY OF HIS GRACE, WHEREIN HE HATH MADE US ACCEPTED IN THE BELOVED."

FIGHT THE GOOD FIGHT OF FAITH

I began reminiscing how Jesus helped me deal with Satan when he came with his temptations, with past homosexual sexual experiences. I still had sexual dreams about men that felt so real. Jesus showed me that I was being tormented by homosexual demons. Reading the word of God reveals that we are fighting evil spirits that are out there to destroy mankind.

According to 2 Corinthians 10:3–5,

> For though we walk in the flesh, we do not war after the flesh. For the weapons of our warfare are not carnal, but mighty through God to the pulling down of strong holds; Casting down imaginations, and every high thing that exalteth itself against the knowledge of God, and bringing into captivity every thought to the obedience of Christ.

God expects us to cast down evil imaginations. When the devil came to me with his temptations by asking me, "Don't you miss having sex with men, and don't you remember the good times," I responded by telling him that he didn't have power over me anymore. I told him I was crucified with Jesus, and that I also died with Jesus, was buried, resurrected, and was seated in heavenly places in Jesus Christ.

I often reminded Satan that he was under my feet. I am no longer his, and I don't belong to myself; I belong to God. I was bought by the power of the cross and resurrection, and I rest in the finished works of Jesus Christ. That I am the righteousness of Christ Jesus, and more than a conqueror, I am what Jesus says I am. My Lord says that I am the light of the world, salt of the earth, and apple of His eye. In the beginning, when I came back to the Lord, I had a bad habit of roaming my eyes. A lot of people have that problem and don't know how to deal with that problem. When I saw a man that passed by me, my eyes and mind would follow him around. I then remember the scripture in Romans 6:13, "Neither yield ye your members as instruments of unrighteousness unto sin: but yield yourselves unto God, as those that are alive from the dead, and your members as instruments of righteousness unto God." The Lord told me to speak to my spirit, soul, body, and that included my eyes and whole body. I looked in the mirror I begin to speak and decree the word over my spirit, soul, body, eyes, and the devil heard the word.

That I, Michael Fernandez, as a new creature: old things are passed away; behold, all things become new. I decreed that I am the righteousness of God and that I am instruments of righteousness not instruments of unrighteousness, and that I am dead to this world but a life onto God. I began casting down every evil imagination. It makes a big difference in how one thinks or speaks and believes in the power of the cross and the resurrection. According to Proverbs 23:7, "For as he thinketh in his heart, so is he." One needs to think about the thoughts that Jesus has toward them and speak them, believe them. According to Psalm 139:17, "How precious also art thy thoughts to me, O God! How great is the sum of them!"

I did the same thing that Jesus did when he was tempted in the desert, I began to fight the good fight of faith, according to 1 Timothy 6:12 (KJV), "Fight the good fight of faith, lay hold on eternal life. Whereunto thou art also called, and hast professed a good profession before many witnesses."

One needs to realize that one needs to submit themselves to God and His word in order to fight the battle of temptation. According to James 4:7, "Submit yourselves therefore to God. Resist the devil, and he will flee from you." I can lay a hand on your head till your hair falls off, you need to believe in the power of the cross and resurrection. We were crucified with Jesus on the cross, and also died with Jesus on the cross and were buried with him by baptism into death, and resurrected with Jesus also set with him heavenly places in Jesus. We need to believe in the finished work of the Lord. This is the scripture I use to fight the good fight of faith: according to Romans 6:1–3,6, "What shall we say then? Shall we continue in sin, that grace may abound? God forbid, How shall we, that are dead to sin, live any longer therein? Know ye not, that so many of us as were baptized into Jesus Christ were baptized into his death? Knowing this that our old man is crucified with him, that the body of sin might be destroyed, that henceforth we should not serve sin."

Don't Believe in the Philosophy of Man

We have seen the vain philosophy of men that are coming into the church teaching the doctrine of the devil. It doesn't matter if they are well-known teachers, if it is not in line according to the word of God, they are false teachers.

As we read the scripture, "And this I say, lest any man should beguile you with enticing words" (Colossians 2:4). Some teachers make them sound like they are very spiritual by quoting or reciting Hebrew and Greek, there is nothing wrong with Hebrew or Greek, it is good that one studies the meaning of the original scripture. But they twist the word of God.

According to Colossians 2:7–8, "Rooted and built up in him, and established in the faith, as ye have been taught, abounding therein with thankgiving. Beware lest any man spoil you through philosophy and vain deceit, after the tradition of men, after the tradition of men, after the rudiments of **the world, and not after Christ."**

This False Teacher Teaches

The Holy Ghost does not convict believers when
they commit sin. Only the sinners.

Let us go to the Word to examine the truth regarding the Holy Ghost. Whether or not he convicts the believer, the Holy Ghost doesn't condemn, but he does convict. We condemn ourselves because of the choices we make.

Viewing the scripture in St. John 16:8 (ISV), "When He comes, He will convict the world about sin, righteousness, and judgment." This false teacher is saying that this verse is not talking to the believer. I couldn't believe what I was hearing. He said the scriptures are only talking to the sinners. I have to disagree. God is talking about all mankind, sinners and Christians.

Let's establish the facts that Jesus said in his Word.

According to John 6:63 (KJV), "The words that I speak unto you, they are spirit and they are life." We established that word of God is also spirit. Another scripture that shows that the Spirit convicts. According to 2 Timothy 3:16 (AMPC), "Every Scripture is God's breath (given by His inspiration) and profitable for instruction, for reproof and conviction of sin for correction of error and discipline in obedience (and) for training in righteousness (in holy living, in conformity to God's will in thought, purpose, and action)."

Here we see from this scripture that the Spirit does reproof, convict, and also correct. This shows that this false teacher is missing the context of the scripture. I do pray for him and ask God to show him the truth regarding His word.

That believers don't need to repent when they commit sin.

Let's continue seeing what the scripture says regarding repenting for the believer.

According to Revelation 3:19 (AMPC),

> Those whom I (dearly and tenderly) love, I tell their faults and convict and convince and reprove and chasten (I discipline and instruct them). So be enthusiastic and in earnest and burning with zeal and REPENT CHANGING YOUR MIND AND ATTITUDE.

Here we see that Jesus Christ is saying that He would tell them of their faults, and convict, reprove, chasten, and cause them to REPENT CHANGING THEIR MINDS AND ATTITUDE. Once again it shows that the false teacher is wrong.

THIS FALSE TEACHER IS SAYING THAT THE BOOK OF 1 JOHN 1:9 IS TALKING ABOUT THE SINNER, NOT TO THE BELIEVERS.

I disagree. Let's look at the scripture: according to 1 John 1:4–5, "And these things write we unto your joy may be full. This then is the message which we heard of him, and declare unto you, that God is light, and in him is no darkness at all." And this verse shows that he talking to believers, not unbelievers. And 1 John 1:9, "If we confess our sins, he is faithful and just to forgive us our sins, and to cleanse us from all unrighteousness."

Even the scripture, Revelations 3:19, shows that Jesus said that he caused his son and daughter to repent.

This false teacher is also teaching that as christians, don't soweth what we reap.

Let's look at some believers in the New Testament (new covenant). Remember their sins are forgiven in the past, present, and future, but when we make the wrong choices in life we are going to reap the consequences of those choices. If someone who is a believer kills someone, guess what is going to happen to that person? Jesus already provided forgiveness for his sin if he repented, but he will still suffer the consequences of the choice he made.

As this believer that lied to the Holy Ghost and how they reap because of their sin. View the scripture according to Acts 5:1–5, 7–10,

> But a certain man named Ananias, with Sapphira his wife, sold a possession, And kept back part of the price, his wife also being privy to it, and brought certain part, and laid it at the apostles' feet.
>
> But Peter and, Ananias, why hath Satan filled thine heart to lie to the Holy Ghost, and to keep back part of the price of the land? 4. While it remained was it not thine own? And after it was sold, was it not in thine own power? Why hast thou conceived this thing I thine heart? Thou hast not lied unto men, but unto God. And Ananias hearing these words fell down, and

gave up the ghost: and great fear came on them that heard these things.

And it was about the space of three hours after, when his wife, not knowing what was done, came in. And Peter answered unto her, Tell me whether ye sold the land for so much? And she said Yea, for so much. Then Peter said unto her How is it that ye have agreed together to tempt the Spirit of the Lord? behold, the feet of them which have buried thy husband are at the door, and shall carry thee out. Then fell down straightway at his feet, and yielded up the ghost: and the young men came in, and found her dead, and, carrying her forth, buried her by her husband.

*How the Judgment Comes Down on Believers in
the Church to Cause Them to Repent*

Another example in my ministry—giving God glory!
I was invited to minister at a church where I had only met the pastor by phone. I didn't know anything about the church, but I agreed to go as a guest minister in his church. As I arrived to minister, the Holy Ghost said to me he was going to show me something and to only speak what I see and what I hear him saying. He told me to call out to a young pregnant woman. As she stood up, I saw a vision over her head. I was able to see her in a bedroom crying because her husband was an evangelist who backslid. The Lord told me to tell her not to worry anymore; He was going to bring him back into ministry. She began to cry. At the time, I didn't know her husband was at the front of the church playing the piano. At the same time, the Holy Spirit began to reveal to me that her father was a pastor. I did not know at the time where I was preaching was at her father's church. It was revealed to me that her father was having trouble in the church. Someone was breaking in and messing up the church by breaking the walls, making holes in the walls, and breaking the furniture. They

didn't know who was doing it. I asked the young woman; she confirmed this was the case. I told her the Holy Ghost was showing me who was causing all this damage to their church. Remember, I was telling her everything I was seeing in the open. Everybody could hear me prophesy to her. I told her the man causing this damage is the landlord who used to be the pastor of that same church. This landlord has backslid and was jealous of your father.

At this time, I didn't realize the landlord was there in the church, hearing this prophecy. I proceeded to tell the rest of what the Holy Ghost was revealing to me. I told them that Jesus wanted the landlord to repent, and if he didn't, in three weeks, he would die of sickness because he brought this upon himself. I don't know why the Holy Ghost didn't have me go directly to the landlord and rebuke him myself. This was the way the Holy Ghost wanted it. As the Holy Ghost continued, she was told to tell her father not to worry anymore; Jesus was going to help him get a red brick church.

As I stopped the prophecy, the pastor came up to me and said, "Brother, that young lady is my daughter, and the young man in the front of the church is my son-in-law, and everything you spoke is true." He said that this night, judgment came on the landlord and that they were planning to announce to the church, at the end of the meeting, they had been granted a loan from the bank to purchase a red brick church building, which no one knew about.

After three weeks passed, the landlord became very ill. He was dying, and he called the pastor and me to confess that he was the one causing all the damage to the church. He asked the pastor to forgive him, and he asked Jesus to forgive him. He was healed. Hallelujah! He came back to Jesus.

THE SINNER'S PRAYER

If you would like to accept Jesus Christ as your Lord, you must believe that Jesus Christ is the son of God and that God has raised

Him from the dead and confess Jesus is Lord according to Romans 10:9: So let us pray,

> Jesus, I believe you are the son of God and that God raised you from the dead and I ask you Jesus to come into my heart and be the Lord of My life, forgive me of all my sins and I repent. Please cleanse me with your precious blood and I confess Jesus Christ as my Lord and Savior. Thank you, Jesus, for forgiving me of all my sins.